So baptism means being with Jesus 'in the depths': the depths of human need, including the depths of our own selves in their need – but also in the depths of God's love; in the depths where the Spirit is re-creating and refreshing human life as God meant it to be.

Rowan Williams, Being Christian

Contents

Introduction	4
About the Authors	6
Acknowledgements	7
Photo credits	8
The 5 Marks of Mission	9
How to use this study guide	11
Study 1 - Heart to heart	14
Study 2 - It passes all understanding	26
Study 3 - We never journey alone	37
Study 4 - Sunday Best	51
Study 5 - The death of gods, the life of God	61
Study 6 - The hospitality of strangers	73
About us	84
Additional ABM resources	85

www.abmission.org

Introduction

The season of Lent has a very clear direction. It leads us to the cross, and in the great Festival of Easter, takes us through death into the joy of the Resurrection.

Good so far, but, once we have arrived on the other side of death, where do we go?

This has always been the question faced by the church. At the Ascension, we are told Jesus commanded us to 'go out into the world to make disciples'. But how? Which direction first? With whom? For how long? Are we there yet?

There are easy, pat answers to these questions, answers grounded in the mission, tradition and theology we have breathed in since we first started to attend church, answers that may have more to do with 'then' than they have to do with 'now'. As with most 'easy' answers, a closer look reveals that each answer contains within it many more questions.

So, let's look at the early church and once again celebrate the passion, enthusiasm, miracles, unity and determination that are so evident in Acts. Surely the answers are there? Perhaps. Or, more likely, in re-reading Acts, we will discover questions and clues about how we might enter into the great adventure of 'mission' in our own time and place. In Australia. Today.

The Acts of the Apostles is most certainly full of wonders. The whirlwind of Pentecost. The growth of the church. The generosity. The healings. The conversions. The beatings. The prison sentences. The deaths. The...

Hang on... the what!?! It's true, Acts tells the story of a brand new church stumbling into being and it's not all pretty. We might prefer Acts preached as triumph and victory, but that's not the half of it.

Evangelists argue, communities are confused, racism rears its head, economics aggrieve, politics pollute. It almost sounds like the real world. Because it was. The real, messy, glorious world of human beings facing massive changes to what they believed and how they were to live. They may have been saints, but they were saints like us.

Mission to a messy, broken world will always be messy and broken mission. That is not to say that it won't be productive, wonderful and glorious as well but...an authentic reading of scripture never suggests one without the other. God's Spirit, the gift of Jesus, working within the eternal Trinity – and with and through us - is more than used to dealing with mess.

For over 150 years, the Anglican Board of Mission has been participating in God's mission in many, varied and *messy* ways. There have been moments of genuine triumph and moments of genuine pain. In both dark days and light, God's Spirit has been present to guide and comfort, advocate and convict, intercede and reveal. Our job has been to listen and to learn, to persevere and to love, to follow and to lead.

We offer these studies - for Lent or for anytime - because we believe that God's mission is an invitation to participate in the adventure of the 'now but not yet' kingdom. A step on the road to forming communities who strive for love, hope and justice.

Whether it be in your home, your church, your suburb or the wider world, the call of mission is the call to be engaged with, to love and to honour all that God has made. We walk the Gospel into the world not simply through words but through our actions. Mission is the continuation of the great Incarnational love story between God and all that God has made.

About the Authors

The Rev'd Canon Stephen Daughtry is Parish Priest of Belair in South Australia and an Education Missioner for ABM. Born in the UK, Steve grew up in Townsville and lived in NSW and the ACT before moving to SA nearly thirty years ago. He began his career as an actor before moving into arts ministry. He was, for twelve years, Artistic Director of Company of Sinners, a theatre company he founded with his partner, Vanessa. Steve worked for ABM for over a  decade, in the areas of Youth, Mission Education and Communications, making over twenty short docos. After working as Media Officer for the Diocese of Adelaide, he was ordained deacon in 2011 and priested the following year. He is a published poet and soccer tragic. Should you ever visit Coopers Stadium, he and Matthew can often be heard singing the praises of referees!

The Rev'd Dr Associate Professor Matthew Anstey: Matthew is a leading Australian Old Testament academic with an international reputation in the area of Biblical Hebrew linguistics. Matthew is Higher Degree Research Program Director at Alphacrucis College, Australia. He is a Research Fellow in the Public and Contextual Theology (PaCT) Strategic Research Centre of Charles Sturt University (CSU), a Visiting Research Fellow in Linguistics, The University of Adelaide, and an Honorary Research Associate Professor (School of Historical and Philosophical Inquiry), University of Queensland. Matthew is also a member of the Doctrine Commission of the Anglican Church of Australia.

Matthew's scholarly interests extend into Biblical Studies and Christian theology. He has published on Genesis, Jonah, Habakkuk, the interpretation of narrative and poetry, scripture, creation, same-sex marriage, and human flourishing.

When not doing academic work, Matthew enjoys cooking, gardening, poetry, music, and coffee and conversation. He lives in Adelaide with Liz and their three children.

Acknowledgements

Matthew and I would like to acknowledge that we are middle-aged, middle-class white guys. And we're clergy! Acts is largely a story written by men, about men - and written at a time when that was the norm. We can't do much about that. What we can do is say that we are deeply convinced that God's story is for all people, regardless of gender, race or sexuality. That's how we read it, despite our innate biases and cultural short-sightedness. That means it's also your story and, because God's story lives in you, you might well disagree with some things we say or suggest. Good! Disagree, name it and give us grief. We seek truth together and no-one is helped if we're always polite. The church grows stronger in a crucible fired by diverse and passionate voices and by disciples seeking to discover what God is up to – and to join in.

We'd like to thank ABM for the invitation to write these studies. The Anglican Board of Mission – Australia is a wonderful organisation and a gift to the wider church, most clearly evident in its willingness to listen voices from the 'edge' and to take necessary and godly risks. Particular thanks to John Deane, the Executive Director, and to the Education Team – the humble but brilliant Brad Chapman, the prophetic and spiky Celia Kemp and the generous, nurturing and passionate Jazz Dow.

And, of course, our love and thanks to Liz and Vanessa. There are no words.

These studies were written at 'Campfire in the Heart' in Alice Springs. We express our gratitude to Sue and David Woods; elders, legends and leaders.

While the book was a collaborative effort and we edited each other's work, the 'A Close Reading' sections are primarily Matt's work and the rest is mostly Steve.

We acknowledge the original custodians of this land and pay our respects to Elders past, present and future; for they hold the memories, the traditions, the culture and the hope of Australia.

Photo credits

The photos used in this study have been taken by ABM staff and volunteers over many years. Thanks to all those who have realised the importance of the visual image in communicating the human condition. Photographers include, among others, Kirsty Robertson, Steve Daughtry, Brad Chapman, Peter Branjerdporn (Anglican Church Southern QLD) and the legendary Don Brice (www.donbrice.com), who transformed the way ABM presented itself with his incredible eye and photographic skill. Most of these photos are from 'the field' and represent communities who have been our Partners in mission.

The 5 Marks of Mission

- Witness to Christ's saving, forgiving and reconciling love for all people
- Build welcoming, transforming communities of faith
- Stand in solidarity with the poor and needy
- Challenge violence, injustice and oppression, and work for peace and reconciliation
- Protect, care for and renew life on our planet

(Anglican Board of Mission - Australia)

The Marks of Mission were originally articulated at the Anglican Consultative Council in 1984 with updates in 1990 and 2012. They are not a final and complete statement on mission but they offer a practical guide to the holistic nature of mission. ABM has translated the Anglican Communion's official Marks of Mission (below) to adapt to our specific context. You might like to have a go at translating the Marks of Mission for your own particular context.

The mission of the Church is the mission of Christ
1. To proclaim the Good News of the Kingdom
2. To teach, baptise and nurture new believers
3. To respond to human need by loving service
4. To transform unjust structures of society, to challenge violence of every kind and pursue peace and reconciliation
5. To strive to safeguard the integrity of creation, and sustain and renew the life of the earth

(Anglican Consultative Council)

How to use this study guide

Step 1. Reading the Scripture
Each study begins with a Scripture reading, which you are encouraged to read together as a group. After the reading, before moving on to the Reflection, take a few moments individually to record or remember your initial response to the text.

Step 2. Reflect
Have one of your group read aloud the 'Reflect' section (or share the reading around the group). This is designed to help you understand the scripture passage contextually, highlighting possible meaning and understanding for you as readers. Feel free to question any of this, see what it sparks in you and ask questions of each other about any ideas raised.

Step 3. Question
The questions are always starting points and every person or group will take them in different ways. That's good! If they're helpful, then go with them. If not, make up your own. Be sure to make space for each person to speak if they wish. Beware of the temptation to dominate a group, as it's rarely, if ever, fruitful.

Step 4. The Marks of Mission
The Marks of Mission are ways in which the church lives out the call of the Gospel. Reflect on this week's 'mark' and read more about the Marks of Mission on page 9.

Step 5. A Closer Reading
This section is designed to allow you to go deeper into the text, understanding it with greater theological and historical depth. You may wish to read this section in parts, sharing the reading and stopping to discuss what is being said. Remember, as always, that you don't have to agree with everything that has been written. Encountering difficult ideas can lead to epiphanies and frustration in equal measure. That's how we learn, that's how the early church learnt! One person in your group may be enraptured while you're bewildered. Talk about it. Be bold.

Step 6. Investigate

Each of the six studies had links (tenuous or strong) to an area of the work of the Anglican Board of Mission – Australia. You might like read about what the Australian Church is doing in Partnership with various people groups and countries.

Step 7. Music

Each week we suggest a song that you can listen to. Up to you of course. They're all available online and can be played on a Smart TV, a Smart Phone or a computer. You might choose to listen as you relax and reflect on the study you have just done or perhaps, you'd like to start with music so as to get your minds into a new place?

Remember...

Lent is a time to CONNECT

Since the fourth century the six weeks prior to Easter were set aside by Christians as a special time of prayer, fasting and reflection. As we spend time together during this Lenten period, we turn our hearts and minds to what Jesus did, not just in the week of His passion, but also in His life and His actions towards others. Lent is a time to CONNECT with Christ, each other and those around us.

Lent is a time to GROW

Above all Lent prepares us for the coming of Easter that we may truly

GROW into the spirit of Easter; to GROW in our understanding and experience of the passion of Christ, the joy of the hope of new life and in our response to the Spirit's call to follow Christ in the world.

Lent is a time to SERVE

It gives us time to reflect on our needs, the needs of others and hence all that we have and do. There has come to be a custom of 'giving up for Lent'. Not only are we called to 'give up for Lent', we are also called to 'take up the Cross' and SERVE the world around us.

Lent is a time to GIVE

The mission of God is always one of giving. Lent reminds us that we are called to live out in the world the self-sacrificing, self-spending life of Christ. As the Easter Community we are free to practice a radical generosity as we GIVE ourselves, in Jesus' name, to each other.

Bible Translations

When doing Bible studies, people often worry about which version they should read. We have chosen to use the text from the NRSV in these studies...but...having a range of translations and versions in your study group will sometimes help you to discover more in the text. Whatever you regularly read will do the job if you invite the Spirit to read with you and don't get too precious about your version being the correct one. Let's always remember that we all read from translations - and no translation can be perfect.

STUDY 1
Heart to heart

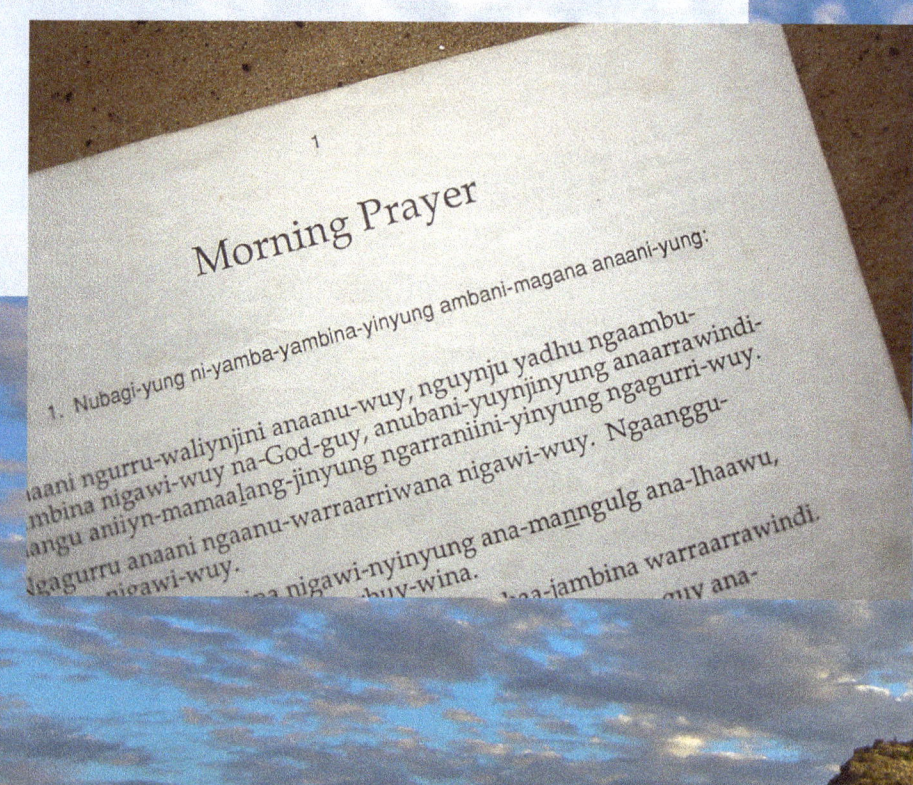

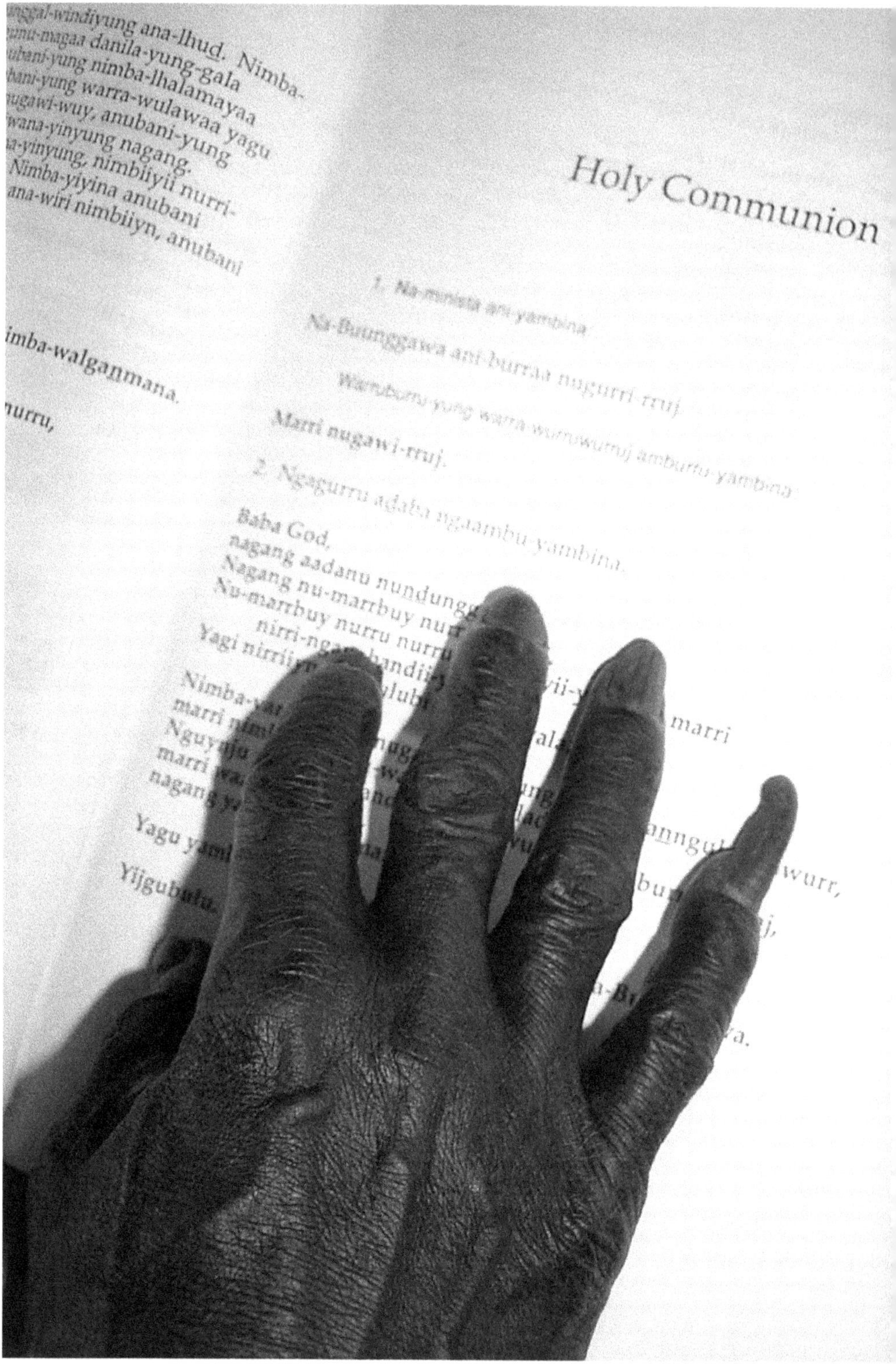

Holy Communion

...nggal-windiyung ana-lhud. Nimba-
...unu-magaa danila-yung-gala
...ubani-yung nimba-lhalamayaa
...ugawi-yung warra-wulawaa yagu
...ugawi-wuy, anubani-yung
...wana-yinyung nagang-
...a-yinyung, nimbiiyii nurri-
...Nimba-yiyina anubani
...ana-wiri nimbiiyn, anubani

...imba-walganmana.

...nurru,

1. Na-minista ani-yambina.

Na-Buunggawa ani-burraa nugurri rruj.

Warnburnu yung warra-wurnuwurnij amburnu yambina.

Marri nugawi-rruj.

2. Ngagurru adaba ngaambu yambina.

Baba God,
nagang aadanu nundung...
Nagang nu-marrbuy nu...
Nu-marrbuy nurru nurr...
   nirri-ngaa...
Yagi nirriiyn...handiiy...

Nimba-va... ...vii-y...
marri nim... ... marri
Nguyiju ... ...ala...
marri wa... ...w...
nagang ya... ...ad...

Yagu yamba... ...anngu...wurr,

Yijgubulu, ...bu... ...j,

... ...a-B... ...va.

Read
Acts 2:1-13

When the day of Pentecost had come, they were all together in one place. And suddenly from heaven there came a sound like the rush of a violent wind, and it filled the entire house where they were sitting. Divided tongues, as of fire, appeared among them, and a tongue rested on each of them. All of them were filled with the Holy Spirit and began to speak in other languages, as the Spirit gave them ability.

Now there were devout Jews from every nation under heaven living in Jerusalem. And at this sound the crowd gathered and was bewildered, because each one heard them speaking in the native language of each. Amazed and astonished, they asked, 'Are not all these who are speaking Galileans? And how is it that we hear, each of us, in our own native language? Parthians, Medes, Elamites, and residents of Mesopotamia, Judea and Cappadocia, Pontus and Asia, Phrygia and Pamphylia, Egypt and the parts of Libya belonging to Cyrene, and visitors from Rome, both Jews and proselytes, Cretans and Arabs—in our own languages we hear them speaking about God's deeds of power.' All were amazed and perplexed, saying to one another, 'What does this mean?' But others sneered and said, 'They are filled with new wine.'

Reflect

"*I don't understand*", is one of the most common experiences of human life.
"*I won't understand*", is equally common - and tragically sad.
"*I will learn to understand*", is a doorway to authentic relationship.

The vast majority of native English speakers in Australia are mono-lingual. Even those of us who have travelled extensively usually find someone who speaks enough English to make us feel understood and welcome. Despite this, many of us have had moments overseas – and at home - when our linguistic ignorance has left us feeling isolated. Standing to one side as people converse, often in more than one language, can lead to feelings of exclusion and inadequacy. When someone opens the door to our inclusion by addressing us in English, we experience being *seen* and valued. If this is difficult for us on an occasional basis imagine what it is like for non-English speaking migrants and refugees during their first months and years in Australia.

The Pentecost experience, for so many of the gathered pilgrims, was probably quite a shock. Perhaps these visitors, migrant workers and traders in Jerusalem spoke enough of one of the local languages to make basic conversation, but to hear people speaking in their native tongue must have felt like a cool breeze on a hot day. Surely, here were people who would understand them, who knew who they were. How odd it must have been to realise that those speaking were *not* their countrymen or women, but foreigners touched by God's Spirit.

How interesting it is that, at Pentecost, God didn't just make everyone able to understand Aramaic. It's almost as if the Spirit of God was openly declaring that the kingdom was no longer bound to one people group but was to become the natural home for all people and all nations and all languages.

How sad that so much evangelism and mission work has reverted to cultural and linguistic imperialism, substituting God's celebration of diversity for a type of monochrome Christianity that resembles the dominant culture of the visitor. A culture that, all too often, has been Caucasian and Western.

Partnership is a word ABM has used for some time now. At the heart of partnership is an understanding that we have to learn the language of those we hope to serve and learn from, especially if we wish to share and learn more of the story of God together. This may prove to be time-consuming, frustrating and difficult – but it is a necessary act of love and respect. It is what God did for us in the full outworking of the incarnation.

Consider this, Jesus never spoke a word of English. He learnt to speak the language of his young mother and brave father, through their patience and deep love for him. When he was older, he used this gift to shed the light of Gospel hope into the darkest places of his inherited culture and religion. He called people, in their own language, into repentance, renewal and new community.

If we wish to love those who speak a different language, be that the language of our beautiful but incomprehensible grandchildren or of a remote village tribe on the other side of the world, may the Spirit of Pentecost guide us to learn before we teach and to recognise the relational power of addressing someone in their heart language.

Question

Share an experience of not being understood. In what ways did you manage to bridge the gap?

Who first made sense of the Gospel in a way you understood?

When someone goes out of their way to help you understand that they respect you and want to know you well, how do you feel? What might that mean for the work of sharing God's great story?

First Mark of Mission
Witness to Christ's saving, forgiving and reconciling love for all people.

A Close Reading

Most of us think that when God enters our lives and draws near to our hearts, we will be full of joy and reassurance and encouragement. We imagine that the presence of God will bring clarity and certainty, order and comfort.

Yet when we read the story of the birth of church, when God enters the lives of the first disciples, the scene presented to us is one of disruption and upheaval.

This disruption occurs at so many levels:

- The "natural order" is overturned as tongues of fire rest on each person without burning them (v 3). Peter fosters this sense of upheaval by talking about the sun turning to darkness and the moon to blood (v 20).

- The usual lengthy and arduous task of learning another language evaporates as people speak foreign languages effortlessly (vv 4-11).
- Norms of sensible social behaviour are cast aside, so that to many onlookers these Jewish disciples appear drunk by breakfast (vv13-15)!
- The religious traditions of that time, privileging one group over another are radically overturned:

    Young people get to participate with old people (v 17)

    Women get to participate with men (vv 17-18)

    Slaves get to participate with free citizens (v 18)

    The spread of God's new life beyond the Jewish people is foreshadowed in the geographical spread of the people groups listed. (This becomes a reality in the chapters ahead.)
- The inescapability of death is disrupted by the resurrection of Jesus (vv 24, 31-32).

Yet this story is not only characterised by upheaval. The fact that Peter interprets what is happening through the lens of Israel's story, in accord with both the ancient prophecy of Joel and with the very recent promise of Jesus (see Acts 1), shows that what is happening was expected at one level. But how it happened, and the full implications thereof, and all that flows from this Pentecost event, was beyond what anyone had imagined.

Interestingly, this strange intermingling of disruption and order is mirrored in the literary form. On the "disruption" side, we observe that Peter improvises quite a bit on the Scripture he cites from Joel:

- He changes "After these things..." (Joel 2:28) to "In the last days...." (v 17)
- He inserts "my" before "slaves", making them God's slaves (v 18), itself a disruptive and provocative claim!
- He adds a whole sentence "and they shall prophesy" to the end of verse 18.

And on the "order" side, a close study of the text shows that Luke structures it using a well-known pattern called a chiasm. Chiasms are literary patterns of A B C... C' B' A', used often in the ancient world to assist with memorisation. And they also allowed one to highlight the centre of a story, which is precisely what Luke does vividly:

    A. "Listen to these words" (v 22a)

        B. God raised Jesus to new life (vv 22b-24)

            C. Scripture reference (vv 25-28)

                D. Resurrection (vv 29-34a)

            C'. Scripture (vv 34b-35)

        B'. God raised Jesus as Lord and Messiah (v 36)

    A'. "They were pierced to the heart" (v 37).

It's as if the irruption of the Spirit is more acutely focussed by placing it within such a constrained literary form. (Incidentally, some scholars see another chiasm inside D above, vv 29-34 – what do you think?).

What then are we to make of this fascinating text and its interweaving of tradition and upheaval, its order and improvisation, its fulfilment and upending of expectations?

It reminds us that when God is among us, truly among us, we might expect there to be

- an integral continuity with what has come before us, as recorded in our Scriptures, our creeds, our traditions, our liturgies, and

- an irruption of new life and unexpectedness into our present context, and

- questions over whether or not this actually is God at work ("they're drunk"!), and

- an obligation to interpret not just our ancient texts, but the present contexts, and

- the ever-radical egalitarian and inclusive Spirit of God, drawing in all those present and in so doing erasing the barriers and boundaries we think are divinely sanctioned, whatever forms they take among us. For Luke, this was around ethnicity and age and gender and citizenship. What are they for your community?

Think

*"And so, if the resurrection of Jesus means the last days have begun, that also means that after the resurrection there's never going to be any new framework, any different way of seeing God in the world. This is it. God and the world are now, you might say, settled in the full and final shape of their relationship. The decisive difference has been made. The end has begun. The kingdom has come. Jesus has advanced out of mere history into God's future. Jesus inhabits God's future fully, so that we who are drawn to be with Jesus in his resurrection are there with him in the future which has already been inaugurated, so that that in itself opens out onto the perspectives that St Paul more than once mentions, of how the Holy Spirit given to us is the foretaste or the down-payment of God's future, the age to come. And so, since this is the beginning of the last phase of human history, since the resurrection of Jesus has made the decisive difference, there's also a sense in which **the destinies of all human beings** are now bound up with Jesus. From now on, every human being finds who they are, who they may be, where they will be, in relation with the figure of Jesus. The future is in his hand and his resurrection gives him that authority. It's described again very clearly in Acts 17 in Paul's sermon in Athens: 'He has set a day when he will judge the world with justice by the man he has appointed. He has given proof of this to all by raising him from the dead.' Once again, the resurrection, the future, the judgement, God's decisive fixing of his relationship with the world is all connected with Jesus and with Jesus' resurrection."*

Rowan Williams – from 'Risen Indeed': The Resurrection in the Gospels

- If, "the destinies of all human beings are now bound up with Jesus", what might that mean for our sense of mission at home and abroad?
- What might Rowan Williams mean when he says, "The end has begun. The kingdom has come. Jesus has advanced out of mere history into God's future"?

Investigate

Read more about ABM's work with Aboriginal and Torres Strait Islander people in the Projects section at **www.abmission.org**

Music

Christ Has No Body Now But Yours (featuring Josh Garrels)
https://www.youtube.com/watch?v=w7ymxW3rndk

STUDY 2
It passes all understanding

> **Read**
> Acts 5:17-42

Then the high priest took action; he and all who were with him (that is, the sect of the Sadducees), being filled with jealousy, arrested the apostles and put them in the public prison. But during the night an angel of the Lord opened the prison doors, brought them out, and said, 'Go, stand in the temple and tell the people the whole message about this life.' When they heard this, they entered the temple at daybreak and went on with their teaching.

When the high priest and those with him arrived, they called together the council and the whole body of the elders of Israel, and sent to the prison to have them brought. But when the temple police went there, they did not find them in the prison; so they returned and reported, 'We found the prison securely locked and the guards standing at the doors, but when we opened them, we found no one inside.' Now when the captain of the temple and the chief priests heard these words, they were perplexed about them, wondering what might be going on. Then someone arrived and announced, 'Look, the men whom you put in prison are standing in the temple and teaching the people!' Then the captain went with the temple police and brought them, but without violence, for they were afraid of being stoned by the people.

When they had brought them, they had them stand before the council. The high priest questioned them, saying, 'We gave you strict orders not to teach in this name, yet here you have filled Jerusalem with your teaching and you

are determined to bring this man's blood on us.' But Peter and the apostles answered, 'We must obey God rather than any human authority. The God of our ancestors raised up Jesus, whom you had killed by hanging him on a tree. God exalted him at his right hand as Leader and Saviour, so that he might give repentance to Israel and forgiveness of sins. And we are witnesses to these things, and so is the Holy Spirit whom God has given to those who obey him.'

When they heard this, they were enraged and wanted to kill them. But a Pharisee in the council named Gamaliel, a teacher of the law, respected by all the people, stood up and ordered the men to be put outside for a short time. Then he said to them, 'Fellow-Israelites, consider carefully what you propose to do to these men. For some time ago Theudas rose up, claiming to be somebody, and a number of men, about four hundred, joined him; but he was killed, and all who followed him were dispersed and disappeared. After him Judas the Galilean rose up at the time of the census and got people to follow him; he also perished, and all who followed him were scattered. So in the present case, I tell you, keep away from these men and let them alone; because if this plan or this undertaking is of human origin, it will fail; but if it is of God, you will not be able to overthrow them—in that case you may even be found fighting against God!'

They were convinced by him, and when they had called in the apostles, they had them flogged. Then they ordered them not to speak in the name of Jesus, and let them go. As they left the council, they rejoiced that they were considered worthy to suffer dishonour for the sake of the name. And every day in the temple and at home they did not cease to teach and proclaim Jesus as the Messiah.

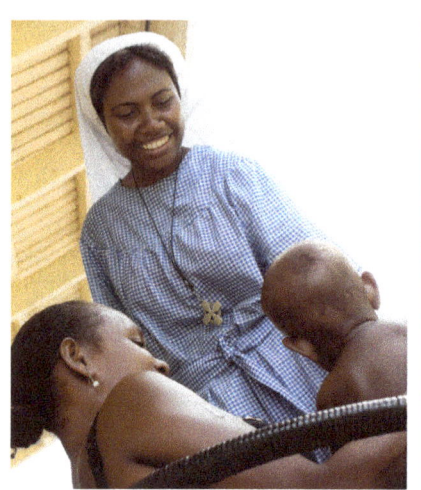

Reflect

Baking heat and sea breezes. Wood smoke from the cooking fires. The laughter of children. Dark, gentle eyes. A war zone.

Sister Dora, a local, was talking to me about the 'Troubles' in the Solomon Islands, in 2003 and before. The Christian Care Centre she worked at was the only domestic violence refuge on the island. She and the other sisters were used to the daily task of 'talking down' enraged husbands and safeguarding women and children in danger. During the 'Troubles' they had been caught on one side of a frontline of fighting. The road to the city – and essential supplies – was closed. In her lilting English and with a broad smile she explained how both warring parties had downed weapons and – with some embarrassment - waved her and the other sisters through all roadblocks, knowing them to be people of peace and faith. Their reputation was their salvation.

It had been so for the Melanesian Brothers (an indigenous Anglican Order) who were negotiating with warlord, Harold Keke. Then Keke's paranoia turned lethal and seven brothers were martyred in an horrific war crime. Peacemaking is not always a safe activity.

In the reading from Acts 5, Gamaliel, a Pharisee, stands between the murderous intent of his colleagues and the Apostles, offering an alternative way forward and, consequently, saving lives. We cannot know his motivations (and various commentators have differing views on this) but his actions prevent bloodshed. Sometimes, whatever our motivations and beliefs, it is our actions and decisions that speak most clearly of how God is at work with and through us.

Our world, especially beyond the borders of Australia, is riven and twisted by war and conflict. Even within Australia, we see communities and groups turning against one another, often cheered on by unscrupulous players who wish to profit, economically or politically, from the conflict they foster. Within our own church, conflict over power and authority threatens our unity. Sometimes it is hard to judge who is in the right and who in the wrong. Sometimes there are no clear answers, except the answer that God's peace and justice might, should we seek to pray for it, to embrace it and to enact it, bring genuine salvation and hope – especially to those who suffer. In the final analysis, peace matters most to those who are victims of violence.

Peacemaking is not an attractive option but an essential vocation. Of course, there are also times in our ever more fast-paced world, when we might also need to allow more time before leaping to judgement.

Christ risked everything in the hope that his life, death and resurrection would reconcile us both to God and to each other. Jesus is the ultimate peacemaker and we are asked to 'follow him' in this calling.

Around the world, ABM's Partners often place themselves in the gap between warring tribes. In the Gaza Strip, the Al Ahli Arab Hospital, run by the Diocese of Jerusalem, stands as a symbol of God's love, offering treatment to all who come. It is a place of peace in the midst of war. Its staff stand with Christ.

Part of the work of 'mission', both abroad and at home, is finding the courage to stand up for those who are the victims of violence, injustice and oppression. In this we must also find the courage to pray earnestly, to trust hopefully and to 'risk' our own reputations for the sake of those who suffer. If the followers of Jesus are not courageous on their behalf, who else shall we expect to fill the gap?

Question

Share experiences of 'standing up for' something or somebody. How did it feel? Was it successful? Would you do it again?

How does your church pursue justice both in Australia and outside?

Are Christians really called to be peacemakers or is that asking too much?

Fourth Mark of Mission
Challenge violence, injustice and oppression, and, work for peace and reconciliation

A Close Reading

This story in Acts contains two well-known statements that are oft-quoted approvingly, one each from the two main protagonists:

Peter says: "We must obey God rather than any human authority".

Gamaliel says: "If this plan or this undertaking is of human origin, it will fail; but if it is of God, you will not be able to overthrow them".

With Peter we have the bold notion that God must be obeyed, irrespective of what any human authority requires, and with Gamaliel we have the equally bold notion that if God is behind an action, then it is unstoppable.

But it doesn't take much reflection to realise that there are in fact issues with both assertions, issues that have played out across the centuries up into the present.

Peter's statement asks, how do we know confidently what God requires? Could we be wrong? And could it be the case that at times, or even as a general rule, God wants us to follow "human authority"? If we think of our local judicial system, or local government, would we not want to obey them as a general rule? For there are more than enough Scriptural and theological reasons to be "good citizens". Paul himself relies on "human authority" on occasion, such as in his appeal to being a Roman citizen when under arrest.

Interpreters of Acts have over the centuries realised that these sort of black and white doctrinal statements raise serious problems. For example, Raymond E. Brown perceptively articulates the dilemma the overall impression of Acts offers to readers:

> *A triumphal picture is painted in Acts. All setbacks are temporary and quickly turn out for good in a Christian movement which is constantly growing numerically... and geographically... On finishing Acts, the reading audience might quite logically have concluded that very soon afterwards the whole world would become Christian... The plan of continuity presented in Luke/Acts is oriented towards the bigger is better; it does not prepare for major defeats or for losses that are not recouped. Such an ecclesiology, when taken in isolation, will leave Christians perplexed when their institutions begin to close, when their churches are being abandoned for lack of members.*

It hardly needs saying that "major defeats" and "losses that are not recouped" are very much part of our current ecclesial experience in Australia.

Similarly, Gamaliel's theology is in fact profoundly problematic. If this actually means that whatever happens is God's will understood in retrospect, then this creates insurmountable problems when bad things happen. Evoking "it's all in the mystery of God" for those times when it doesn't make sense hardly seems like a coherent account of God's action in the world, and sounds more like fatalism than responsible engagement and participation in God's world. Abraham Kuyper articulates this problem most acutely:

> It is not true that God the Lord destroys forthwith that which is not from Him and crowns with success every endeavour of all His believers.... How is it that Gamaliel's advice, so profoundly untrue, is repeated again and again in life? Could it not be just as well the other way around, that to have no success suggests virtue? ... Oppressed, downtrodden, molested—can these not be signs that you are walking on the way of God?[1]

Even the text itself raises questions about Gamaliel's advice, for the two exemplars he offers both ended with the dispersion and scattering of the followers (vv 36-37). So perhaps his appeal convinced his colleagues because they read "between the lines"?

What then does this mean for us, reading this text in the twenty-first century, and for our mission? In a way, this text reminds me of Job's friends. If you study what they said, it is hard to find anything ostensibly wrong in what they said, yet God says they spoke wrongly. The common problem is the idea that what is true of a particular situation is then thought to apply to all situations. Yes, there are times when obeying God means opposing empire. Yes, there are times when each of us say, "This came about because God willed it". But these statements don't apply to all situations at all times. Each context, each culture, each moment requires discernment, faith, trust, possibility. This makes our journey of faith much more challenging, but also much more interesting and open-ended.

So really challenging Scriptures like Peter and Gamaliel (texts that scholars to this day have wildly different opinions about!) are good to read, they are important to read, because life is really challenging, mission is really challenging, discerning God's will is really, really challenging.

[1] *Revisie der revisie-legende* (1879); English translation in G.C. Berkouwer. *The Providence of God* (Studies in Dogmatics; Grand Rapids: Eerdmans, 1952). pages. 173-74.

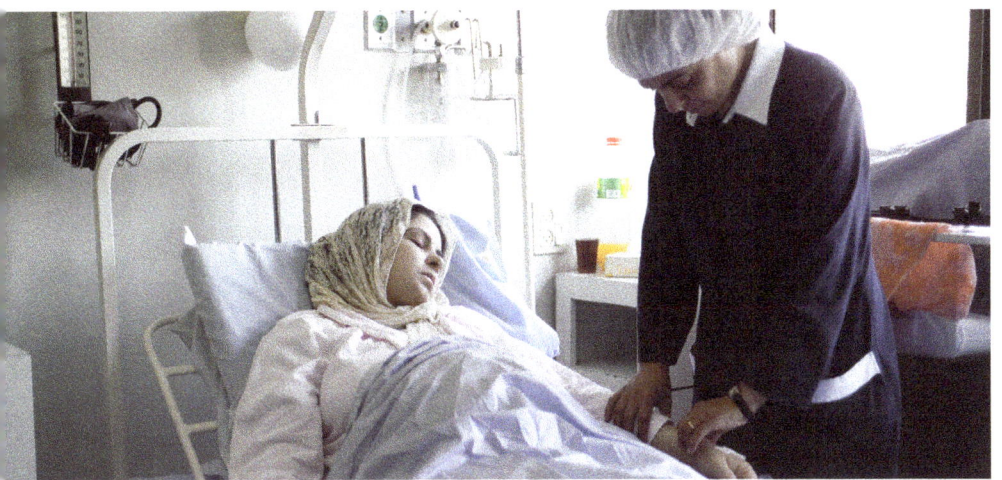

Think

"Did I offer peace today? Did I bring a smile to someone's face? Did I say words of healing? Did I let go of my anger and resentment? Did I forgive? Did I love? These are the real questions. I must trust that the little bit of love that I sow now will bear many fruits, here in this world and the life to come." **Henri Nouwen**

- Peacemaking often begins in our own homes and churches. When we fail in the small things, resentment can build walls between those who were previously friends. Have we experiences of that happening to us? Have we experiences of dismantling walls and restoring relationship?

- Is Henri Nouwen right to suggest that, *"the little bit of love that I sow now"*, will actually bear fruit?

- Ask each other, when have there been times when you've found it impossible to know God's will? We think you'll be surprised by the stories you share together.

Investigate

Read more about our Partnerships with the Solomon Islands and the Holy Land in the Projects section at **www.abmission.org**

Music

Ben & Micah Hester, 'By The Riverside' https://youtu.be/WTfPLK_ub7E

STUDY 3

We never journey alone

Read
Acts 8:26-40

Then an angel of the Lord said to Philip, 'Get up and go towards the south to the road that goes down from Jerusalem to Gaza.' (This is a wilderness road.) So he got up and went. Now there was an Ethiopian eunuch, a court official of the Candace, queen of the Ethiopians, in charge of her entire treasury. He had come to Jerusalem to worship and was returning home; seated in his chariot, he was reading the prophet Isaiah. Then the Spirit said to Philip, 'Go over to this chariot and join it.' So Philip ran up to it and heard him reading the prophet Isaiah. He asked, 'Do you understand what you are reading?' He replied, 'How can I, unless someone guides me?' And he invited Philip to get in and sit beside him. Now the passage of the scripture that he was reading was this:

'Like a sheep he was led to the slaughter,
   and like a lamb silent before its shearer,
      so he does not open his mouth.
   In his humiliation justice was denied him.
      Who can describe his generation?
      For his life is taken away from the earth.'

The eunuch asked Philip, 'About whom, may I ask you, does the prophet say this, about himself or about someone else?' Then Philip began to speak, and starting with this scripture, he proclaimed to him the good news about Jesus. As they were going along the road, they came to some water; and the eunuch said, 'Look, here is water! What is to prevent me from being baptized?' He commanded the chariot to stop, and both of them, Philip and the eunuch, went down into the water, and Philip baptized him. When they came up out of the water, the Spirit of the Lord snatched Philip away; the eunuch saw him no more, and went on his way rejoicing. But Philip found himself at Azotus, and as he was passing through the region, he proclaimed the good news to all the towns until he came to Caesarea.

Reflect

I woke one morning in an earth floored hut, high in the Cordillera Mountains of the Northern Philippines. As I stepped from the door, I had the almost mystical experience of discovering myself above the cloud line. Crisp mountain air and extraordinary vistas of treed peaks emerging from the whipped egg white of clouds. The day assembled itself and the village shuffled into life. I'll never forget that moment. Or the day that followed.

As I wandered around, smiling and waving, beginning to understand the rhythms of another world, I was struck again and again by the apparent simplicity, beauty and very tactile nature of rural poverty. Almost everything that is done is an action; a touch, a lift, a leading, a blow. The machines and mechanisms that dictate most of my world were missing.

It was then that I saw the girl on the verandah. Young, probably adolescent, profoundly disabled. She was tied at the wrist with a long piece of thick string attached to the verandah post. I imagine this was to keep her from straying too far. An elderly villager (again, I imagine, it was a relative) kept watch and cared for her. This was her life and the best care she could expect. The best those who loved her could manage in the midst of their own struggle to survive. She was not abandoned nor was she able to access any of the services or care that might improve her life.

I was shocked by the string that held her in place. I was shocked by the lack of options she and her family had. I was amazed by the care the village gave her. I was profoundly ashamed that her circumstances were so far removed from the (relative) wealth of resources Australians might expect. *(And this is in no way to underestimate the inadequacy of disability resourcing in our own country).*

When I was young, I dreamed of the ability to fly. Sometimes, as an adult, I would like the power to perform miracles. If that were the case, I could have prayed over this girl and she would have been healed. Everything would have been alright. Correct? Probably not. God is not ours to command. Had the miracle occurred, I would, no doubt, have felt better – and very godly too. But the village would have remained poor and all the ramifications of that would have continued to play out in people's lives. Miracles are God's province and I welcome them, but they are not band-aids for our conscience.

The reason I was there was to see a grain mill that ABM had helped fund, after local, Filipino, Anglican clergy and development workers had spent months talking with the village to ascertain what would assist them most effectively. The grain mill was the miracle, one built on patient, disciplined,

loving relationship. The machine meant hours less work each week for many; hours that could be spent in leisure, in community building, in caring for the ill and the disabled. The machine meant greater profits for the farmers and the intangible benefit of the knowledge that someone on the other side of the world cared about this far-flung village. Inclusion, renewal and hope were at work. Here was my miracle. I was simply a witness.

Escaping poverty is the path to social restructure that allows resources to be made available for the poorest of the poor. Communities that flourish together tend not to forget their weakest members.

In that moment, I felt as if I were the Ethiopian Eunuch and the village was Philip, mysteriously appearing along my journey explaining to me what the fulfilment of scripture meant. I felt that I had been baptised into a new understanding of how God was present and at work in redeeming the world through the mission of the church, both imminent and transcendent.

Too often, our desire to 'fix' every immediate problem can make us unable to grasp the broader picture of what is really going on. We need to recognise that, while sometimes we might be encouragers and guides, at other times we must be encouraged and guided. To stand in solidarity with the poor it is important that we learn what poverty is and does – and that we show the humility to recognise the areas where our own resources are meagre and in need of replenishment.

Authentic mission will always rely on the principles of respect, trust, and humility, guided by the work and Word of the living God.

Question

Have you ever been tempted to 'fix' a problem just so that it will go away?

Can you remember a time when you thought you were helping but ended up being helped?

Are you willing to share an experience of being 'led' by the Spirit to a person or place and realising afterwards how important that leading was in your life?

Third Mark of Mission
Stand in solidarity with the poor and needy

A Closer Reading

Philip is going about his business, when an angel of the Lord tells him to go to a desert road. He sees a eunuch in a chariot. A eunuch is a man, who as a boy before puberty, has had, at the least, his testicles removed. It was a humiliating and dangerous procedure, often fatal.

The eunuch was returning home from worshipping in Jerusalem, reading Isaiah.

The Spirit tells Philip to go up to the chariot. Philip runs up to the chariot and asks, "Do you understand what you are reading?" Philip, as does God, comes alongside and listens.

The eunuch replies: "How can I understand unless someone guides me?" The respectful approach of Philip begins a conversation.

The story continues. "And the eunuch invited Philip to get in and sit beside him."

Christians all too often invite themselves in, barging in with brochures, launching a monologue. We fail to see the deep contradiction between our hostile methods and the hospitable God we want to talk about. How can a God of love and freedom be shoved down someone's throat?

But here, the eunuch, in response to Philip's respectful attitude, invites Philip into his space.

And so we come to the haunting Isaiah text that the eunuch is reading:

> *"He was led like a sheep to the slaughter,*
> *and as a lamb before the shearer is silent,*
> *so he did not open his mouth.*
> *In his humiliation justice was denied him.*
> *Who can speak of his descendants?*
> *For his life was taken from the earth."*

The eunuch is reading about a man who suffered terribly, in silence. A man who was humiliated and denied justice. A man without descendants.

In other words, a man *just like a eunuch*.

Eunuchs were castrated without their consent, humiliated, with no hope of descendants.

The Ethiopian eunuch identifies deeply with the suffering man described in Isaiah. This raises his curiosity: who was Isaiah talking about?

He asks: "About whom, may I ask, does the prophet say this, about himself or about someone else?" Who could this person be with whom I identify? Surely not a god, surely no one worships a humiliated god?

"And Philip, starting with this scripture, tells the eunuch the good news about Jesus." Starting with this scripture, the eunuch's scripture, Philip tells the eunuch about Jesus, the lamb who was slain.

The eunuch probably saw himself in the story of Isaiah, but imagine his surprise when he saw Jesus in *his* story, in all its suffering and heartache.

The story continues: As they were going along the road, they came to some water and the eunuch asked yet another question, "Look, here's some water! What's to stop me from being baptised?"

The eunuch orders the chariot to stop, and they both go into the water where the eunuch is baptised.

In baptism the eunuch comes to belong to God and God's people and God's story.

I want to make three missional reflections on this story:
Respect, Trust, and Humility.

Respect

Philip, for only a brief period, joins the eunuch's journey, enters his chariot, listens to his story, reads his texts, answers his theological questions, baptizes at his request, and then leaves him be, never to see him again.

The integrity of the eunuch's journey is respected from beginning to end.

For a brief time, he is accompanied by Philip, a stranger, who obeyed the Spirit's promptings.

So Luke tells this as a story of two journeys, which overlap ever so briefly. But in a beautiful narrative detail, Luke records three things that they do together:

> *they travel together* along the road,
> *they go down together* into the water,
> *they come up together* from the water.

So, for a brief moment, two lives align perfectly. Although the Eunuch's journey is never disrespected, it is a journey like no other. For he now belonged to Jesus.

So, respect doesn't mean keeping a permanently polite distance.

Mission that is in accord with the hospitable love of God is not airy-fairy content-less mush. Rather, it involves profound conversation centred on God's Son.

Trust

There is no anxiety here. It is mission premised on the massive *priorness* of God's love and grace towards us. We too often anxiously wonder where the unchurched, the dechurched, the mischurched are to be found. Yet Philip did not know where the Eunuch was, who the Eunuch was, or anything about the Eunuch's openness to meeting Jesus.

We are not to be anxious about the where or who or how or why – we need to be attentive to the Spirit's guidance and ready to join another's journey, to be a midwife for newborn faith in Jesus.

Humility

The Ethiopian was a eunuch, but also a government heavy-weight. He was the Treasurer! He knew all about power and influence and wealth.

So was God like his boss, the Queen of Ethiopia, or like him, the castrated one? To his and our great surprise, it is the latter. God is the Lamb who was slain, who remained silent, who suffered injustice, refusing to defend himself.

As Balthasar puts it so beautifully:

God revealed who God is, in becoming everything that is not God, by pouring himself out into the world he created, by emptying himself into suffering human existence, corrupted by death and alienated from God.[2]

2. Balthasar p461, vol 1, Glory. Cf. vol 2, p.12

Think

"There is another world, and it is this one". **Paul Eluard**

- How might the work of God's mission be enhanced by the church learning to speak and act with greater *respect*, acknowledging that many people are seeking God and that all people must be met at a level that enhances their dignity?

- How might the work of God's mission be enhanced by the church engaging in that mission with a greater sense of *trust* that God is truly with us, however we may perceive ourselves or the circumstances?

- How might the work of God's mission be enhanced by the church learning to speak and act with greater *humility*, acknowledging that Jesus saw no reason to step away from the lowliest of paths and the poorest of companions?

Investigate

Read more about our Partnership with the Philippines in the Projects section at **www.abmission.org**

Music

The Porter's Gate - Little Things With Great Love
https://www.youtube.com/watch?v=pm5VQAxdMrc

STUDY 4
Sunday Best

**Read
Acts 11:1-18**

Now the apostles and the believers who were in Judea heard that the Gentiles had also accepted the word of God. So when Peter went up to Jerusalem, the circumcised believers criticized him, saying, 'Why did you go to uncircumcised men and eat with them?' Then Peter began to explain it to them, step by step, saying, 'I was in the city of Joppa praying, and in a trance I saw a vision. There was something like a large sheet coming down from heaven, being lowered by its four corners; and it came close to me. As I looked at it closely I saw four-footed animals, beasts of prey, reptiles, and birds of the air. I also heard a voice saying to me, "Get up, Peter; kill and eat." But I replied, "By no means, Lord; for nothing profane or unclean has ever entered my mouth." But a second time the voice answered from heaven, "What God has made clean, you must not call profane." This happened three times; then everything was pulled up again to heaven. At that very moment three men, sent to me from Caesarea, arrived at the house where we were. The Spirit told me to go with them and not to make a distinction between them and us. These six brothers also accompanied me, and we entered the man's house. He told us how he had seen the angel standing in his house and saying, "Send to Joppa and bring Simon, who is called Peter; he will give you a message by which you and your entire household will be saved." And as I began to speak, the Holy Spirit fell upon them just as it had upon us at the beginning. And I remembered the word of the Lord, how he had said, "John baptized with water, but you will be baptized with the Holy Spirit." If then God gave them the same gift that he gave us when we believed in the Lord Jesus Christ, who was I that I could hinder God?' When they heard this, they were silenced. And they praised God, saying, 'Then God has given even to the Gentiles the repentance that leads to life.'

Reflect

Parish Notice for St Matthews, Hadley Ridge, South Australia:
As you all know, the bishop will be visiting next Sunday and we want to make a good impression. It is our custom that the men will dress traditionally and proudly wear their penis gourds. Gentlemen, please each bring a lethal weapon and I will ask Brian and Atticus if they would ceremonially attack the bishop as she attempts to enter the building. She is a woman of stout heart and strong faith so don't go easy. We'll all have a good laugh if you can make her flinch. Ladies, please wear your Mothers Union skirts and, on this occasion, go topless. Bras are acceptable but not really traditional, given the spirit of the occasion, however, we move with the times. A rousing rendition of Amazing Grace accompanied by loud drumming and energetic dancing as the Bishop enters the building please. Mark, I trust that you will be able to slaughter a pig to lay across the threshold for the bishop to walk over. I will be very upset if we are pig-less for this important occasion. Normal rosters for readers, sides-people and morning tea. Don't let me down as I would hate for the parish to be embarrassed.

Picture this event in your own parish (and we recognise that it may not be a pretty picture!) then reflect on the outrage it would cause. Conversely, in certain parts of Papua New Guinea this type of welcome is normal, culturally appropriate behaviour - and completely acceptable.

Whose cultural norms are 'right' and 'godly'? Do sausage rolls, fairy cakes and cups of tea better represent a Christian welcome than a mumu.³

For many of us, cultural 'norms' are accepted without even having to think about it. We generally believe that we 'know' the right thing to do. Often, it is only when we are dislocated through travel or circumstance – as Peter was when asked to visit Cornelius in Ceaserea – that we have to re-examine our cultural models and question what we have always seen as 'right and good'.

People groups have cultures, families have cultures, schools and workplaces have cultures. It is entirely possible to find that we are engaged with vastly different cultures at home and at work. That means we're all living cross-culturally. Every person involved in cross-cultural mission, be that in another country or within our own community, is challenged – as Peter was. We are challenged to examine ourselves and our dominant culture and to practice the humility necessary to understand and learn and discover the gifts of the host culture. The solid ground of genuine Christian community is the willingness to pray, listen to and learn about those we consider as 'different', finding ways to welcome and be welcomed into the family of God.

3. Look it up, there's a great recipe here: https://www.tokpisin.info/mumu-papua-new-guinea/

Question

In your own life, what cultural barriers have you encountered? What have you challenged and what have you been able to accept?

Have you ever discovered the joy of moving from seeing someone as 'the other' to naming them as your friend?

What cultural norms, practised in your own church or community, might be disconcerting for a visitor? Can these be examined, acknowledged and changed in order to build a more welcoming community, one open to the new and different?

Second Mark of Mission
Build welcoming, transforming communities of faith.

A Close Reading

It is hard for modern Christian readers of Acts 11 to grasp how momentous this moment is in the life of the church, given that religious dietary regulations are unfamiliar to most of us. These rules were not simply part of their religious tradition, they were embedded in the Scriptures and were a powerful unifying symbol of the identity and cohesiveness of the Jewish people. Still today, *kashrut* for many Jewish believers and *halal* for Muslims are central to religious practice and identity.

So how did the early Christian community come to change its mind about this matter?

To answer this, we need to pay attention to what we can identify as six different forms of "testimony" and how each testimony is evaluated and checked for authenticity.

I suggest you read the passage again carefully and ponder each of these in turn. I've bolded each testimony and underlined its corresponding evaluation:

1. **Reportive testimony** - "the believers... heard that the Gentiles had also accepted the word of God" (v. 1). The remarkable inclusion of the Gentiles is reported, yet the report is not taken as accepted, for they "<u>criticise</u>" Peter and demand an explanation.

2. **Narrative testimony** - Peter then tells a story from his own life, his own witness to the report (v. 4). The entire telling of the story is evaluated after it is told, with the outcome being that the Jewish Christians "<u>were silenced and praised God</u>" (v. 18).

3. **Revelatory testimony** - within Peter's story, he recounts the famous vision of the clean and unclean food (vv. 5-10). So those listening not only have to reckon with his story, but his witness to God's revelation via the dream. Interestingly, in the telling of this, Peter notes that <u>he himself disputed</u> the "voice from heaven" three times, as he couldn't believe what was being revealed.

4. **The Spirit's testimony** - Peter then goes on to recount how the Holy Spirit spoke directly to him to go with the men who arrived (v. 12). That this was in fact the Spirit is then confirmed when the man they visit says an angel had told him to expect Peter's visit and to receive his gospel message (v. 13)!

5. **Embodied testimony** - Peter shares how the Spirit had "fallen upon" the Gentile believers, "just as it had upon us" (v 15). That is, there was a manifestation in their lives of the Spirit that was just like Peter's. This manifestation demonstrated the authenticity of their conversion.

6. **Scriptural testimony** - Peter then remembers the words of Jesus, yet even here, there is a clear sense of evaluation when Peter says, "Who was I that I could hinder God?" (v. 17).

What we see here is actually a very sophisticated and intricate story by Luke that captures the dynamic process by which the Jewish Christians came to change their mind. Note how the story is not actually about the abolition of the food laws, but about the inclusion of the Gentiles in the people of God. To agree to this watershed change, this break from tradition and all that was familiar and agreed upon for thousands of years, they took into account a raft of evidence, and evaluated each in turn. It is the combination of these forms of knowing and discerning and their coherence, their "hanging together", that leads to the massive rethink about the Gentile's inclusion among the people of God.

The Jewish church in Acts did not simply "change its mind", it discerned what it believed to be the will of God in their contemporary context. And the multiplicity of testimonies and means of discernment evidenced in this story is a model for us about how to discern the mind of Christ in our context.

Every generation of Christians faces this dilemma and must ask, "Is what we've always done actually the will of God?" Whether it be around slavery or the equality of women or inter-racial marriage or divorce or capital punishment or contraception or environmental stewardship or human sexuality, the Spirit is amongst us, testifying through story and memory and Scripture and lived experience - and even visions and dreams.

And like the Jewish church, perhaps we too need, unexpectedly, to come to that place of "silence and praise", where the boundaries of the world we were so certain were fixed by God forever are expanded or erased in ways beyond our current imagination.

Think

"If a work of art is rich and vital and complete, those who have artistic instincts will see its beauty, and those to whom ethics appeal more strongly than aesthetics will see its moral lesson. It will fill the cowardly with terror, and the unclean will see in it their own shame." **Oscar Wilde**

- Have you ever seen or appreciated something in a completely different way to someone else? Do you understand why? What did you do next?

- What sort of 'mission' projects are you most likely to undertake or support? How do you think your choices are affected by your personality, your values, your culture or biases? How might we best discern what God is calling us to work with and support?

Investigate

Read more about Newton Theological College, PNG in the Projects section at **www.abmission.org**

Music

Carrie Newcomer, 'You Can Do This Hard Thing'.
https://www.youtube.com/watch?v=bHxRsSSeNBo

STUDY 5

The death of gods, the life of God

> **Read**
> Acts 17:16-34

While Paul was waiting for them in Athens, he was deeply distressed to see that the city was full of idols. So, he argued in the synagogue with the Jews and the devout persons, and also in the market-place every day with those who happened to be there. Also, some Epicurean and Stoic philosophers debated with him. Some said, 'What does this babbler want to say?' Others said, 'He seems to be a proclaimer of foreign divinities.' (This was because he was telling the good news about Jesus and the resurrection.) So they took him and brought him to the Areopagus and asked him, 'May we know what this new teaching is that you are presenting? It sounds rather strange to us, so we would like to know what it means.' Now all the Athenians and the foreigners living there would spend their time in nothing but telling or hearing something new.

Then Paul stood in front of the Areopagus and said, 'Athenians, I see how extremely religious you are in every way. For as I went through the city and looked carefully at the objects of your worship, I found among them an altar with the inscription, "To an unknown god." What therefore you worship as unknown, this I proclaim to you. The God who made the world and everything in it, he who is Lord of heaven and earth, does not live in

shrines made by human hands, nor is he served by human hands, as though he needed anything, since he himself gives to all mortals life and breath and all things. From one ancestor he made all nations to inhabit the whole earth, and he allotted the times of their existence and the boundaries of the places where they would live, so that they would search for God and perhaps grope for him and find him—though indeed he is not far from each one of us. For "In him we live and move and have our being"; as even some of your own poets have said,

"For we too are his offspring."

Since we are God's offspring, we ought not to think that the deity is like gold, or silver, or stone, an image formed by the art and imagination of mortals. While God has overlooked the times of human ignorance, now he commands all people everywhere to repent, because he has fixed a day on which he will have the world judged in righteousness by a man whom he has appointed, and of this he has given assurance to all by raising him from the dead.'

When they heard of the resurrection of the dead, some scoffed; but others said, 'We will hear you again about this.' At that point Paul left them. But some of them joined him and became believers, including Dionysius the Areopagite and a woman named Damaris, and others with them.

Reflect

"And when I asked little Lisa where eggs and milk come from, she said, 'From the shop!', and she had no idea about farms at all!" Ah, for the good old days when we all milked the cow and gathered the eggs and... washed clothes by hand and cut wood for the stove and died early of curable diseases... ok, not all good I suppose.

What we may have lost is the sense that the land we lived on and in was deeply important. We once needed to care for it so it would care for us. Industrial farming and the national and international transit of goods have led us far from any sense of our reliance on, and appreciation of, the gift of place God has given us. No wonder so many – especially younger people – are searching for something more authentic, sourcing local produce and talking about 'food-miles' in relation to what they buy.

Of course, in so many places on earth, people still rely on the capacity of the land on which they live to sustain life. As the climate changes and regular seasons fluctuate, terror grips communities as they struggle to plan for cropping and survival.

I watched in Kenya as a single engineer led a group of villagers in building an ABM-funded sand-dam across the local river. Sweating men wielded sledgehammers, smashing slabs of rock from the sides of the river. Those slabs were carried away on improvised stretchers of bound branches, then placed into the dam wall. Women mixed concrete in 40 degree heat. No-one was getting paid. The dam was the payment. Come the monsoon season the river would flood, sand would build up against the dam wall and millions of litres of water would be trapped in that sand. The sand stops the water evaporating. Foot pumps would then move the water from shallow sand wells to newly terraced gardens and people would eat until next cropping season. Assuming that the rains did come. These were people who truly knew their land, their climate... and their vulnerability.

When Paul spoke in the Areopagus and invoked the 'unknown' God, naming Yahweh as the source of all life, he made it clear that God did not live in man-made edifices. Paul also alluded to the fact that our 'boundaries', our allotted spaces, within the created order might help us to 'grope towards God – even though God is not far from us'. Many indigenous people recognise God *in* the *boundaries* of the land. Western Christians, however, are often enslaved by the idea that our lives have no boundaries. Our Areopagus is filled with temples to the car, the international flight, the bank account, the shopping mall, the property portfolio and the quick fix – to comfort, security and relaxation. Should these 'gods' of ours die, we would once again have to rely on the land on which we live. In this time of climate change and over-consumption, the worship of our current 'gods' is alienating us from Yahweh, killing the land and poisoning the futures of many of the world's most vulnerable.

Perhaps, in this time of Lent, - or anytime - we might be called to repent of our exploitation of God's created gift, changing our attitudes and actions so that life might flourish. If we refocus our hearts and minds, seeing God in the all that God has made, perhaps we will not only honour God more fully but also reclaim that sense of place which grounds us in wonder. Wonder that we are 'made' in love and for a purpose.

Question

The Bible doesn't mention climate change so why should we care about it? Discuss.

Do we need to repent of our exploitation of the natural world? What form might that repentance take?

Might learning to love the creation, spending time in and with nature, and seeking the good of the whole created order, bring us closer to Yahweh, who, "gives to all mortals life and breath and all things"?

Fifth Mark of Mission
Protect, care for and renew life on our planet.

A Close Reading

We only have two speeches recorded in Acts by Paul to an entirely Gentile audience, here and earlier in Lystra (14:15-17). Paul's speech here is clearly intended to be persuasive, starting with a compliment: "Athenians, I see how extremely religious you are in every way!" (v 22).

What he says next though is both surprising and insightful: "For as I went through the city and looked carefully at the objects of your worship, I found among them an altar with the inscription, 'To an unknown god.' What therefore you worship as unknown, this I proclaim to you."

It's clever because it is good pedagogy: I once had a Hebrew lecturer, Professor Bruce Waltke, who described his experience of studying Semitic

languages at Harvard University as "going from the unknown to the unknown" – in other words, it was very difficult! He said learning occurs rather when we go "from the known to the unknown", and this is Paul's strategy here.

And it's surprising for modern readers because too often we restrict God's revelation to what is found in Scripture or in the church. Yet these very Scriptures testify to God's witness being found in an entirely "non-Christian" environment! (And perhaps some of us doubt that some people could be worshipping God outside all that we would name as Christian?)

Paul takes this further in the next part of his speech, by stressing the universality of God's reign: God made all things, gives life and breath to "all mortals... and all things", oversees "all nations on the earth" and for this purpose: that they might "perhaps grope for him and find him" (NRSV v 27).

It is striking how Paul then brings his argument to a culmination not with a Scriptural text but with one of their own philosophers, Aratus (c. 315-240 BCE): "For we too are his offspring", taken from the opening lines of his poem Phaenomena:

> Let us begin with Zeus, whom we mortals never leave unspoken. For every street, every market-place is full of Zeus. Even the sea and the harbour are full of this deity. Everywhere everyone is indebted to Zeus. For we are indeed his offspring...

Seeing the broader context of this quotation deepens our understanding of what Paul is arguing, for in effect Paul says, "Let us begin with God (and not Zeus!)".

Moreover, this is not his only allusion to ideas found in literature known to his listeners. Scholars have noted other possible allusions to Greco-Roman philosophers such as Cicero, Aeschylus, Marcus Aurelius and Epictetus. For example, in verse 25 Paul says God is in need of nothing, alluding to Euripides' (c. 480-406 BCE) play *Herakles*:

> *Dear friend, all these things you said are side issues. ...I don't believe that the gods engage is such unholy relationships, nor have I ever believed this story about gods tying up their parents in chains and I won't believe it now. Nor can I ever believe that one god is the lord of another. A god, if he is a real god, is in need of nothing (1345-1346).*

And similarly, Paul in verse 28 is probably quoting Epidemes' work *Cretica* (c. 700-600 BCE), in which Minos the Cretan says to Zeus (yes, Zeus again!):

> *They fashioned a tomb for you, holy and high one,*
> *Cretans, always liars, evil beasts, idle bellies.*
> *But you are not dead: you live and abide forever,*
> *For in you we live and move and have our being.*

I have included these citations from the thinkers that Paul cites because when one grasps the degree to which Paul engages with them, one sees much more clearly how Paul is in fact building his argument. More importantly, it challenges us to rethink how we undertake mission in the twenty-first century.

For too often Christians are wary of engaging with contemporary thinkers (philosophers, scientists and artists) and ideas and have been convinced they must "quote the Bible" to make an argument valid. Yet, if the people at the Areopagus had no knowledge of the Jewish Scriptures, what would Paul have proved by quoting them? And the point is, isn't our contemporary situation very often like Paul's, given the lack of biblical literacy is so endemic?

Like Paul, we need to end up with the resurrection, as this is the punch-line of the gospel. God in Christ conquered death. Like Paul, we too must live with the range of responses to this scandalous claim: some will scoff, some will want a further conversation, and some will come to believe (vv 32-33).

But surely being scoffed at, or being invited back for more debate, is better than speaking in a way that simply makes no sense at all?

Think

"Teach the children. We don't matter so much, but the children do. Show them daisies and the pale helatica. Teach them the taste of sassafras and wintergreen. The lives of the blue sailors, mallow, sunbursts, the moccasin-flowers. And the frisky ones – inkberry, lamb's-quarters, blueberries. And the aromatic ones – rosemary, oregano. Give them peppermint to put in their pockets as they go to school. Give them the fields and the woods and the possibility of the world salvaged from the lords of profit. Stand them in the stream, head them upstream, rejoice as they learn to love this green space they live in, its sticks and leaves and then the silent, beautiful blossoms.

Attention is the beginning of devotion."

Mary Oliver, from her essay, "Do you think there is anything not attached by its unbreakable cord to everything else?"

- How often do we take the time to sit still and examine the world in which we live? How is the Lord of all creation speaking to us through the gift of what has been made?

- At a time of climate emergency, how might the church advocate for the life of the planet, the just and responsible use of creations' gifts and the future of our children? Does it matter?

Investigate

Read more about our Partnerships with Kenya and Zambia in the Projects section at **www.abmission.org**

Music

Playing For Change, 'What a Wonderful World'
https://www.youtube.com/watch?v=ddLd0QRf7Vg

STUDY 6

The hospitality of strangers

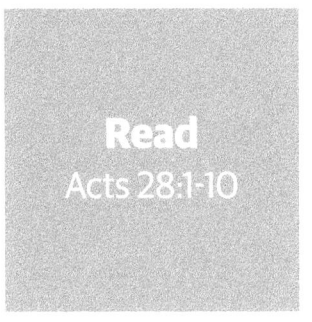

Read
Acts 28:1-10

After we had reached safety, we then learned that the island was called Malta. The natives showed us unusual kindness. Since it had begun to rain and was cold, they kindled a fire and welcomed all of us round it. Paul had gathered a bundle of brushwood and was putting it on the fire, when a viper, driven out by the heat, fastened itself on his hand. When the natives saw the creature hanging from his hand, they said to one another, 'This man must be a murderer; though he has escaped from the sea, justice has not allowed him to live.' He, however, shook off the creature into the fire and suffered no harm. They were expecting him to swell up or drop dead, but after they had waited a long time and saw that nothing unusual had happened to him, they changed their minds and began to say that he was a god.

Now in the neighbourhood of that place were lands belonging to the leading man of the island, named Publius, who received us and entertained us hospitably for three days. It so happened that the father of Publius lay sick in bed with fever and dysentery. Paul visited him and cured him by praying and putting his hands on him. After this happened, the rest of the people on the island who had diseases also came and were cured. They bestowed many honours on us, and when we were about to sail, they put on board all the provisions we needed.

Reflect

Sitting at the back of the classroom is not a new experience to me. That's where you're most likely to get away with things, as every school-kid knows. It's also the safest place if you're not sure quite what's going on. Sitting at the back of a classroom at Wontulp-Bi-Buya College[4] in Cairns was, for me, more of the latter than the former.

At Wontulp, Aboriginal and Torres Strait Islander people study the sacred texts of both the Bible and the Dreaming, talking about where God has been in their history, is now - and what God is calling us to in the future. I was both silenced and captivated as I watched people wrestle with what it means to be a follower of Christ and a traditional owner of the story and land we call Australia. I, quite rightly, had nothing to contribute but my attention. This was deep and serious mystery.

The Book of Acts is the story of two people groups, Jews and Gentiles (and in fact, both of these had many sub-groups), who, when brought into contact with the strangeness and joy of the Gospel story, were challenged to bring what they had known of God together with what was being revealed to them. Nothing about that process could have been easy or straightforward. Like all new births it was a mixture of the sharpest pain and the most profound happiness.

Acts is so often preached and taught as 'triumph' and yet our lived experiences are often of struggle and misunderstanding (and such are also lurking beneath the surface of Acts everywhere for the attentive reader). What was revealed in the life, death and resurrection of Jesus demanded the deepest, most honest and most demanding examination of what had been, what was and what might be emerging. The message of the Apostles may have been 'Good News' but the implementation of that news tore people apart, personally and communally. Something new was entering the world, with all the associated blood, tears and laughter.

What has been so remarkable in the Australian journey, is the way so many Aboriginal and Torres Strait Islander people have been so receptive to the Gospel despite the incredible levels of cruelty and dispossession they faced. Realities that we are only just allowing ourselves (in the non-indigenous community) to recognise. What is also amazing is the level of hospitality and patience that indigenous people have shown towards the people and religion that has caused so much hurt for so many.[5] Perhaps it is time for us to listen much more carefully to the Indigenous Church?

When Paul is shipwrecked on Malta, the people there show spontaneous, generous and innate hospitality. When Paul is bitten by a snake – and then survives – they try and interpret what has happened through the lens of their belief structure and systems. When Paul starts to heal, they accept this gift with enthusiasm. But there is no mention of Paul preaching to them - or of mass conversion - even though it is difficult to believe that Paul ignored that opportunity! As Paul sails away, the people of Malta are left to ponder the arrival of this new view of God, the meaning of the miracles of healing and the conundrum of how to integrate the new and prior understandings.

As an Australian church, have we ever really examined for ourselves what it might mean to 'be' the church in this country, instead of simply relying on imported understandings of ecclesiology, spirituality and tradition? Have we ever really understood what God was doing here before our European ancestors arrived? Have we listened deeply to the voice of Indigenous people who have both ancient and fresh understandings of faith? At some stage, all of our ancestors have had to grapple with the question about new and old wineskins. Perhaps the deep work of 'mission' is sometimes to unsettle and to stir examination of where God has been with us, where God is now and what God is asking today. Perhaps the question of 'mission' is always, **'where do we go from here'?**

4. http://wontulp.qld.edu.au/about_thename.php

5. For a deeper understanding of this history, please read ABM's publication 'A Voice in the Wilderness' by Celia Kemp. www.abmission.org/voice

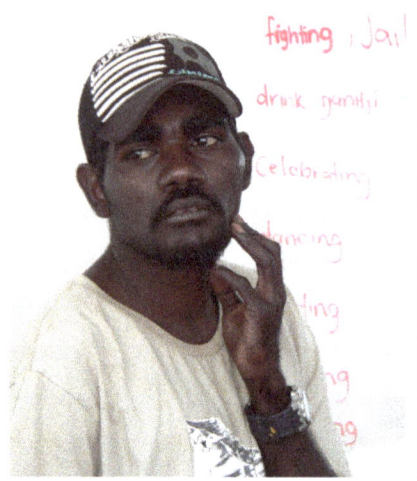

Question

Share ways in which the Gospel of Jesus has caused you to examine your own cultural or family values. Are there those in your group who have never experienced any difficulty? Are there others who have had to really struggle to find a way forward?

Have you ever met anyone you would identify as truly 'holy'? What impact did they have on you? Were you challenged to change after the encounter?

Another imperative of mission

"The marginalised in society are the main partners in God's mission. Marginalised, oppressed, and suffering people have a special gift to distinguish what news is good for them and what news is bad for their endangered life.

In order to commit ourselves to God's life-giving mission, we have to listen to the voices from the margins to hear what is life-affirming and what is life-destroying…"

From: Together Towards Life: *World Council of Churches Affirmation on Mission and Evangelism*

A Close Reading

All of us have encountered a different culture at one time or another, be it through work, travel or moving to a new location. Sometimes it's a new subculture we've heard of but don't know and sometimes it's a brand-new culture with a different language. What happens when people from different cultures meet?

Anthropologists have long described such encounters between two different cultures in terms of *host* and *guest*. The visitor/outsider is a guest and must receive the hospitality of the host in order to be welcome among them.

In the complex exchanges that occur when guests and hosts meet, many dynamics are at work. A key goal of these interactions is to find a common ground, a shared understanding and knowledge of expected, forbidden, and permissible actions. Ideally, this shared understanding will include matters of morality (what is acceptable for both of us), religion (who are our gods), value (what matters for both of us), symbols (what means what) and so forth. Another goal is to negotiate the three main phases of interaction: welcome, stay, and farewell.

The consequences of getting this wrong can be everything from embarrassing (though guests do allow hosts to make mistakes not normally accepted – and vice-versa) to catastrophic, as recounted in George Thompson's book, *How to Get Along with Your Church*, which tells the story of a new minister in a parish whose welcome, stay and departure totalled less than seven days (!):

Arriving there a few days before his first worship service, the eager graduate drove to the church building. ...An old gnarly tree off to the side of the structure virtually prevented use of the only side door. Clearly, here was a moment to prove himself, the pastor thought.

Driving to the church parsonage, he unpacked some things until he found his chain saw. He returned to the church building and immediately cut down the tree, cleaned up the limbs and twigs, and painted the door. In less than a week, this brand new pastor was heading off to a different [parish]. Why? Because ... John Wesley, founder of the Methodist movement [had planted that tree!][6]

Clearly, being cognisant of host and guest dynamics is central to mission, and the short vignette in Acts 28:1-10 gives us a stellar example of this, narrated through the eyes of the guests.

The welcome (vv 1-2) is notable for three of the words used:

The natives showed us unusual kindness. Since it had begun to rain and was cold, they kindled a fire and welcomed all of us round it.

The word "natives" is *barbaroi* in Greek and is translated in various ways: islanders (NIV), native people (ESV), barbarous people (KJV), barbarians (ASV). Isn't it often the case that even knowing how to name those we encounter cross-culturally is challenging?

The phrase "unusual kindness" in Greek is more like "not a regular kindness", where kindness is *philanthropian*, "love of persons". The NRSV translation is misleading, because the hosts'

6. Page 93.

welcome is not *unusual* but rather something more like "extraordinary" (NASB). They went out of their way to welcome Paul and his colleagues. Isn't this often our experience of encountering new cultures, in which lavish hospitality is shown?

The word "welcomed" is actually a more ordinary word meaning "receive" or "take aside". And isn't this so vital, to be welcomed, received, placed inside the circle as it were?

This succinct verse captures some of the dynamics of this moment of encounter. And reading it this way brings to life a tiny detail (v 3): "Paul had gathered a bundle of brushwood and was putting it on the fire" (!!!). Can you see now the significance of this? Paul had accepted the welcome and was participating reciprocally in the encounter.

And then, another tiny, but significant detail, brought to light through the lens of cultural anthropology: "a viper, driven out by the heat, fastened itself on his hand". This tells us that the locals had a pre-existing communal fire ready for guests (and other events of course) that was extremely large! So this was not a "let's makes a fire on the beach" moment, rather, they had been taken into the heart of the community to the central source of heat, warmth, and light.

This is also of course the crisis point and here the clash of worldviews is evident. The locals interpret the snake bite as divine retribution and await his demise. Try to picture the tension of this period of time: "They were expecting him to swell up or drop dead, but after they had waited a long time and saw that nothing unusual had happened to him, they changed their minds and began to say that he was a god". And from this extraordinary miracle (for surely the locals knew the viper was poisonous), further hospitality is offered by a local elder, Publius, whose father was dying. Paul, we discover, not only avoided snake bite death, he brought God's healing to the father and all the unwell locals.

But what is most striking of all is that there is no mention of conversion or preaching. That said, it is easy to imagine that the God in whose name Paul prayed lodged in the hearts and minds of these people more deeply than any words would have done. Given all the verbosity narrated in Acts, perhaps this is Luke's way of gently reminding us that there is so much more to mission than preaching.

Think

"*I actually believe that we Christians can lead the way in our nation's healing, if we face our own truth. We, as Christians, are by nature, people of reconciliation. In Christ, God was reconciling the world to God's self, not counting our trespasses against us, entrusting the message of reconciliation to us (2 Corinthians). As Christians we have no fear of truth. We know the power of forgiveness. We know the power of reconciliation. And we know the power of healing. We are people of Good News and hope, yet this all springs from an honest facing of our personal and collective histories. Jesus says, in his Sermon from the Mount, "When you're offering your gift at the altar, if you remember that your brother or sister has something against you, leave your gift before the altar and go. First be reconciled to your brother or sister, and then come and offer your gift". If you remember that your brother or sister has something against you. The uncomfortable truth, the starting place for reconciliation, begins with acknowledging Australia's first peoples, our brothers and sisters, have something, indeed, against this nation....and our church. If we remember...? Leave your gift before the altar and go. Be reconciled with your brother and sister. Where do we begin? Firstly, listen to the stories of Australia's Aboriginal and Torres Strait Islander peoples. The first peoples. Become acquainted with the full history of our nation. Not the edited version, or the version we like the best, or the version that makes us feel good – but the whole story.*" **Bishop Chris McLeod, National Aboriginal Bishop in the Anglican Church of Australia**[7]

- Consider how the unfinished business of reconciliation that Bishop Chris speaks about might be important to address if we want to move forward as a truly 'Australian' church?

- Jesus suggests that worship can only truly happen when we are reconciled? Do you believe this? What will God's mission look like in your own community?

Investigate

Read more about our Partnership with Wontulp-Bi-Buya College in the Projects section at **www.abmission.org**

Music

Gurrumul, 'Jesu' - https://youtu.be/N4LiJiiSlf8

7. https://www.youtube.com/watch?v=LJ71vPR_2L4

About us

ABM is the national mission agency of the Anglican Church of Australia working with overseas and Aboriginal and Torres Strait Islander people and communities.

We have a holistic view of God's mission. We work with Anglican Church partners and others to see lives empowered and transformed spiritually, materially and socially.

We help the Anglican Church and the wider community realise and respond to the invitation for all to be a part of God's hope for the world.

ABM believes in a world where all people enjoy God's promise of love, hope and justice. We work to see this belief become a reality.

....

Anglican Board of Mission - Australia Ltd ABN 18 097 944 717
Local Call: 1300 302 663 | International: +61 2 9264 1021
Enquiries: info@abm.asn.au | www.abmission.org

Additional ABM resources

Into the Desert

40 days of Scripture readings, reflections and prayers that take you on a spiritual journey into the Australian wilderness.

Available as an app or an 88-page booklet at

www.intothedesert.org

Songs from a Strange Land

Beautiful words and images to take you from Advent to Epiphany with a particular emphasis on Indigenous Christianity, the Australian landscape and Creation theology.

Available as an app or a 158-page booklet at

www.songsfromastrangeland.org

A Voice in the Wilderness:
Listening to the Statement from the Heart

(with the art of the Rev Glenn Loughrey)

A study to open up conversations about the theological response to the Statement from the Heart, available as a free pdf or to purchase as a book at:

www.abmission.org/voice

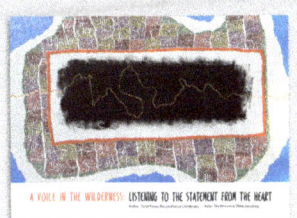

Deep calls to Deep App

(Easter)

A 46-day journey into the mystery of suffering that begins in Holy Week and ends on Ascension Day.

These free apps for iPhone and Android devices available at:
www.abmission.org/apps

Copies of this booklet can be obtained by contacting ABM or at
www.abmission.org/lent

Publication info

Scripture quotations are from New Revised Standard Version Bible: Anglicized Edition, copyright © 1989, 1995 National Council of the Churches of Christ in the United States of America. Used by permission. All rights reserved worldwide. http://nrsvbibles.org

"Our waking life's desire to shape the world to our convenience invites all manner of paradox and difficulty. All in our custody seethes with an inner restlessness. But in dreams we stand in this great democracy of the possible and there we are right pilgrims indeed. There we go forth to meet what we shall meet."

Cormac McCarthy, *Cities of the Plain*

www.ingramcontent.com/pod-product-compliance
Lightning Source LLC
Chambersburg PA
CBHW040243010526
44107CB00065B/2858